H is for Hoosier

An Indiana Alphabet

Written by Cynthia Furlong Reynolds

Illustrated by Bruce Langton

Sleeping Bear Press
310 North Main Street
Chelsea, MI 48118
www.sleepingbearpress.com
1-800-487-2323

Sleeping Bear Press is an imprint of The Gale Group, Inc.
a division of Thomson Learning, Inc.

Printed and bound in China.

10 9 8 7 6 5 4 3

Library of Congress Cataloging-in-Publication Data

Reynolds, Cynthia Furlong.
H is for Hoosier: an Indiana alphabet / by Cynthia Furlong Reynolds.
p. cm.
Summary: The letters of the alphabet are represented by words, set in short rhymes
with additional information, relating to the state of Indiana.
ISBN 1-58536-041-4
Indiana—Juvenile literature. 2. English language—Alphabet—Juvenile literature.
[1. Indiana. 2. Alphabet.] I. Title.

F526.3 R49 2001
977.2—dc21   2001042892

D is for Dedication and F is for Friends

This book is dedicated to the many friends
who have encouraged me and enriched my life,
who have carpooled and carried extra loads when I had deadlines,
and who believed that I had a book or two within me—
even when I doubted it. My heart-felt thanks!

CYNTHIA

For my sons Brett and Rory, you make the sun shine every day for me.
To Rebecca, my loving wife who gives me the motivation
and drive to be not only a better artist but a better person.

My thanks to Sleeping Bear Press and Cynthia Furlong Reynolds
for all their hard work in bringing this book to life.

Finally, my thanks to Alyssa, Ashley, Charlie, Michael,
Rory, Ryan, and Stephanie, the children illustrated in this book.

BRUCE

A begins the Alphabet and the word Amish too, you know.
The Amish live like farmers did 200 years ago.
Horses pull the plows as they till the ground,
and horses pull their wagons all around the town.

The Amish own more than 3,600 farms in Indiana. Their roots go back to the 16th century when a Dutch priest named Menno Simons left the Catholic Church.

The Amish live and work the way farmers did in Indiana's early years without electricity, telephones, and automobiles. Horses pull their plows, wagons, sleighs, and carriages. Up to several generations can live together in one large house. At night people gather around the stove to read and tell stories.

Indiana has the third largest population of Amish in the U.S.

B b

B can be for Basketball,
a sport for Hoosiers, short or tall.
They pass and play, dribble and dunk
into the hoop where the orange ball is sunk.

Indiana is renowned for its basketball tradition. No state has produced more great players, coaches, or heart-rending stories of victory and defeat. Hoosiers enthusiastically adopted the game shortly after physical education instructor Dr. James Naismith invented basketball in Springfield, Massachusetts in 1891.

The Basketball Hall of Fame in New Castle captures the magic of "Hoosier Hysteria." The Hickory Huskers' gym in Knightstown was used for the filming of the movie "Hoosiers." In Indiana, the high school state championship tournament is considered a premier sporting event.

The Cardinal is a brilliant red bird that whistles clear, pleasant songs that sound like *what-cheer, cheer, cheer*; *purty-purty-purty*; or *sweet-sweet-sweet*. To warn their mates of danger, they sound a *chip...chip*.

Cardinals live year-round in Indiana. Adult cardinals measure eight to nine inches long. Although the male has a bright red cap and coat, the female isn't as brightly colored, allowing her to blend into thickets where she sits on her nest. Cardinals build cup-shaped nests lined with twigs, leaves, and fine grass. The mother lays three or four pale blue-spotted eggs, and the father helps feed and protect the babies. Look for cardinals along the edges of woods, near brushy swamps, and in your backyard.

Cardinal starts with the letter C.
Our state bird whistles cheerfully.
You'll know him by his bright coat of red,
from the tip of his tail to the top of his head.

Indiana's famous sand dunes cover 15,000 acres on the southern shore of Lake Michigan. Listen closely and you'll hear the "singing sands," a ringing sound that is caused by pressure and friction of bare feet against quartz crystals in the sand.

The dunes were created thousands of years ago when glaciers moved during the last ice age. The dunes change constantly as northwest winds blow sand back and forth. The oldest dunes sit farthest from Lake Michigan. Mount Baldy is the largest dune in Indiana at 123 feet high. It moves between four and five feet southward from the lake every year.

D stands for the Indiana Dunes.
Along Lake Michigan's shores they glisten.
Singing sands are what you'll hear
if you just walk and listen.

In 1679, French explorer Robert Cavelier, called Sieur de la Salle (1643-1687), traveled down Indiana's St. Joseph and Kankakee rivers looking for a water route to the Pacific Ocean. The next year, La Salle explored northern Indiana before heading down the Mississippi River to the Gulf of Mexico. He claimed all the lands he explored for France.

In 1803, famous American explorers Meriwether Lewis and William Clark met in Clarksville (Indiana Territory) to prepare for the launch of their expedition through the American Northwest.

Ee

Explorer begins with the letter E.
Explorers came from across the sea,
searching for gold treasures and glory.
Their adventures make an exciting story.

Ff

F salutes our Flag, waving free.
Around a torch symbolizing liberty,
circles of stars fly
across a blue sky.

In honor of Indiana's centennial in 1916, the Daughters of the American Revolution held a contest to design a state flag. Paul Hadley of Mooresville won the challenge, and in 1917 Indiana adopted this flag.

The blue and gold banner contains many symbols. The torch stands for liberty and enlightenment. The rays represent liberty's far-reaching influence. Count the stars that circle the torch. Each star stands for the one of the 13 original colonies. The five stars inside the outer circle symbolize the next five states to enter the Union. Look for the largest star, the 19th, which sits just above the torch's flame. This star represents Indiana, the 19th state, which we believe is the best and brightest star!

Virgil (Gus) Grissom

The Grissom Air Museum in Peru is dedicated to the memory of the first Hoosier in outer space, Virgil ("Gus") Grissom (1926-1967).

Born in Mitchell, Grissom was a member of the first team of U.S. astronauts to fly for the National Aeronautics and Space Administration (NASA). In 1961, he became the second American to enter space. Six years later, he died while training for a moon flight.

Historic military aircraft are lined up in military precision outside the Grissom Air Museum. You can see the B-17 Flying Fortress, a rare B-58 nuclear bomber, and the A10 Warthog. Inside the museum, look for jet engines, missiles, survival gear, war prizes, and other military memorabilia.

G greets Grissom Air Museum
and the astronaut with the same name.
He was the second American to fly so high;
in outer space he gained his fame.

Did you know that...

H is for Hoosier.
What is a Hoosier? You may ask.
There are many different ideas,
so giving an answer is a difficult task.

Indiana is called the Hoosier State and its people are known as Hoosiers, although historians don't really know why. They do, however, have several different ideas about the origins of the famous nickname.

In Cumberland, England, the word *hoozer* meant anything unusually large. But how could that apply to Indiana? Others say the name is taken from a man named Samuel Hoosier who liked to hire workers from Indiana. Many believe that the word once was part of a slang expression, such as "Who's yer?" for "Who's here?" Or perhaps it means "Husher" for someone who could hush or calm a brawl.

Before Indiana was settled, the slang word was used in the 13 colonies to mean "a frontiersman, countryman, rustic."

Whatever its origin, the word *Hoosier* referring to an Indiana resident first appeared in print in 1826.

Originally called Fall River, this swampy little settlement on the shallow White River was renamed Indianapolis in 1821. "Polis" means city, so Indianapolis stands for "the city of Indiana." The new settlement became the state capital in 1825 because of its central location.

Indianapolis quickly developed into the state's largest city thanks to the arrival of the National Road in 1834, the Central Canal in 1839, and the railroad in 1847.

Look at a map of Indianapolis and you will see that it looks like a wagon wheel, with the Soldiers' and Sailors' Monument at the hub. Indianapolis has many fun places to visit, among them the world's largest Children's Museum, Eiteljorg Museum of American Indians and Western Art, the homes of poet James Whitcomb Riley and President Benjamin Harrison, and the Indiana State Museum.

I stands tall for Indianapolis,
the capital of our state.
This is where the rules and laws are made
that make our state so great.

Jonathan Jennings starts with **J**.
Our first governor, the history books say,
helped choose our capital and write our laws.
He made Indiana's statehood his special cause.

Jonathan Jennings

1784 ★ 1834

Indiana became a state largely through the efforts of Jonathan Jennings. As the territory's first representative to the United States, the Charleston resident petitioned Congress to admit Indiana to the Union as early as 1812.

On December 11, 1816, Indiana became the 19th state, with 64,000 residents. They chose Jonathan Jennings as Indiana's first governor.

In 1822, Governor Jennings retired as governor and traveled to Washington, D.C. to serve in the U.S. House of Representatives. Jennings County is named after him.

J j

The 1886 discovery of natural gas in Kokomo launched Indiana's industrial age. By offering free gas and land, Kokomo attracted enterprising businesses, entrepreneurs, and inventors. Among them was Elwood Haynes, who invented stainless steel. But Kokomo remembers Mr. Haynes best for inventing America's first gasoline-powered automobile, which made its trial run July 4, 1894. Indiana's once-thriving automobile industry was launched that day. Studebaker and Dusenberg cars were also made in Indiana.

One of Indiana's most poetic place names, Kokomo was named for a Miami Indian chief who might have been mythical. A pioneer named David Foster offered 40 acres of land to build the Howard County seat here. In exchange, he asked to name the town after Chief Kokomo.

Kokomo was also home to John Powell, developer of the first mechanical corn picker. Kemp Brothers Canning Company developed the first canned tomato juice here too, in 1928.

Kokomo carries the letter K.
This city's name is fun to say!
People came here from near and far
to see Elwood Haynes drive his gas-powered car.

Did you know that one of our best-loved presidents grew up in Indiana? Abraham Lincoln (1809-1865) moved to Indiana when he was seven and spent his boyhood here. He later wrote, "We reached our new home about the time the State (of Indiana) came into the Union."

The world's largest collection of Lincoln memorabilia is displayed at the Lincoln Museum in Fort Wayne. You can visit Lincoln's boyhood home in Spencer County.

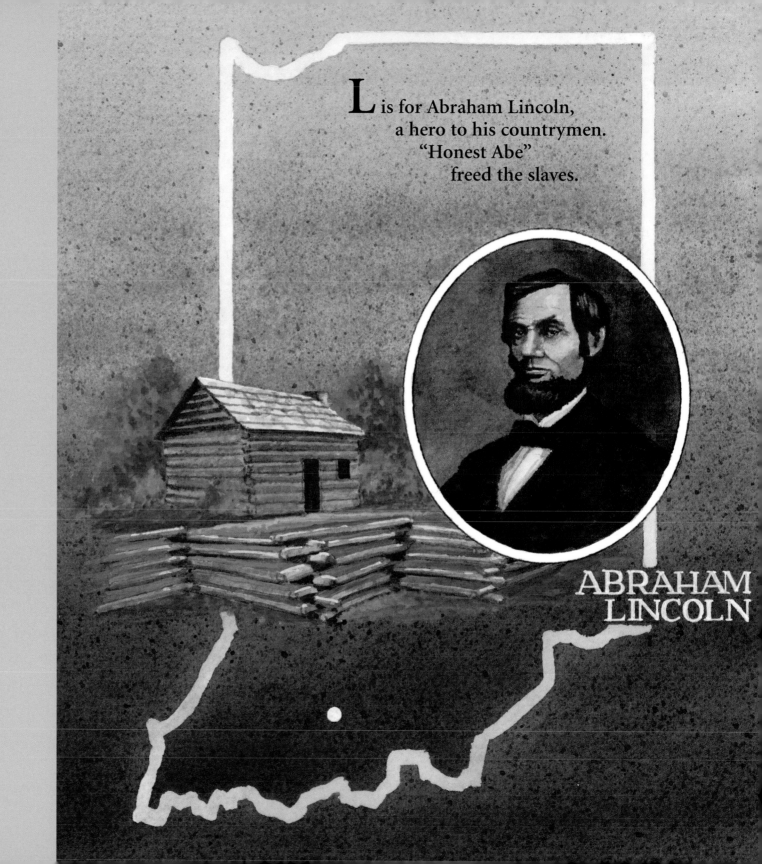

L is for Abraham Lincoln,
     a hero to his countrymen.
     "Honest Abe"
          freed the slaves.

ABRAHAM
LINCOLN

In 1911, Indiana's automotive industries launched the world-famous Indianapolis 500 automobile race. They built the Indianapolis Motor Speedway, a two and one-half mile track where visitors still watch fast cars zoom 200 times around. That is a total of 500 miles! The first winner averaged 75 miles an hour. Now the average speed is over 167 miles an hour.

The Indianapolis Motor Speedway races have inspired important automobile improvements such as the invention of rear-view mirrors, balloon tires, and the development of ethyl gasoline.

The Indianapolis Motor Speedway hosts another big car race every summer called The Brickyard 400.

M is for Motor Speedway,
the place to be on Memorial Day,
when fast cars race around the track
200 times before they come back.

500

n
N
N

Natives and Name both begin with N.
Our Natives, who gave us our Name,
fished and hunted in the "Land of Indians"
long before explorers and pioneers came.

Indiana means "Land of Indians." Twenty-three tribes lived on Indiana's lands, beginning with the prehistoric Mound Builders, who created forts and villages 15,000 years ago. The Woodland culture lived here from 500 B.C. until 1000 A.D. Later, the Mississippi culture established large towns, including Angel Site on the Ohio River.

When Europeans discovered America, Indiana was home to Miamis, Weas, Potawatomis, Piankashaws, Delawares, and Shawnees. Nowadays, fewer than 8,000 of our residents are natives.

O

The wide and winding Ohio River starts in Ohio and then runs along Indiana's southern border, separating us from Kentucky.

Following in the footsteps of European explorers, French woodsmen called voyageurs paddled the Ohio's waters as they hunted and trapped animals. Indiana's earliest pioneers crossed the river from Kentucky into Indiana and carved out farmland from thick forests. Later, riverboats steamed up and down the waters. Now coal is shipped down the river in barges.

Indiana's lowest point sits at the

O is for a river called Ohio.
Along Indiana's southern border, its waters flow.
Voyageurs hunted animals here long ago,
and pioneers crossed the river in sunshine, rain, and snow.

The glorious, spicy scent of our state flower, the peony, fills the springtime air here in Indiana. Victorians called these spring blooms the flower of "bashfulness," but they aren't bashful in taking root. Early pioneer women loved planting peonies, a hardy plant that can live longer than a century. That is why Indiana has so many.

Some peonies have single flowers, others have double blooms and their colors can range from blood-red to carmine, pink, and white. Although they usually grow to be three feet tall, they can reach a height of 12 feet.

P p

P is for Peony, which gives us
one of spring's sweetest smells.
Kneel on your knee, sniff and see
the flowers colored in scarlet and pastels.

Quayle starts with **Q**.
This vice president is a Hoosier, too.
Dan Quayle's museum shows his worldview
and honors all other vice presidents, too.

DAN QUAYLE

Dan Quayle became our 44th vice president when George H. Bush was elected into office in 1988. Born in Indianapolis in 1947, Dan Quayle served four years.

Indiana has sent five vice presidents to Washington, D.C. Mr. Quayle followed in the footsteps of Schuyler Colfax (1823-1885), Thomas Hendricks (1819-1885), Charles Fairbanks (1852-1918), and Thomas Marshall (1854-1925). Indiana's vice presidents, as well as 40 others, are honored at America's only vice presidential museum, which is located in Huntington. At the museum you can see exhibits, memorabilia, and videos about all of America's vice presidents.

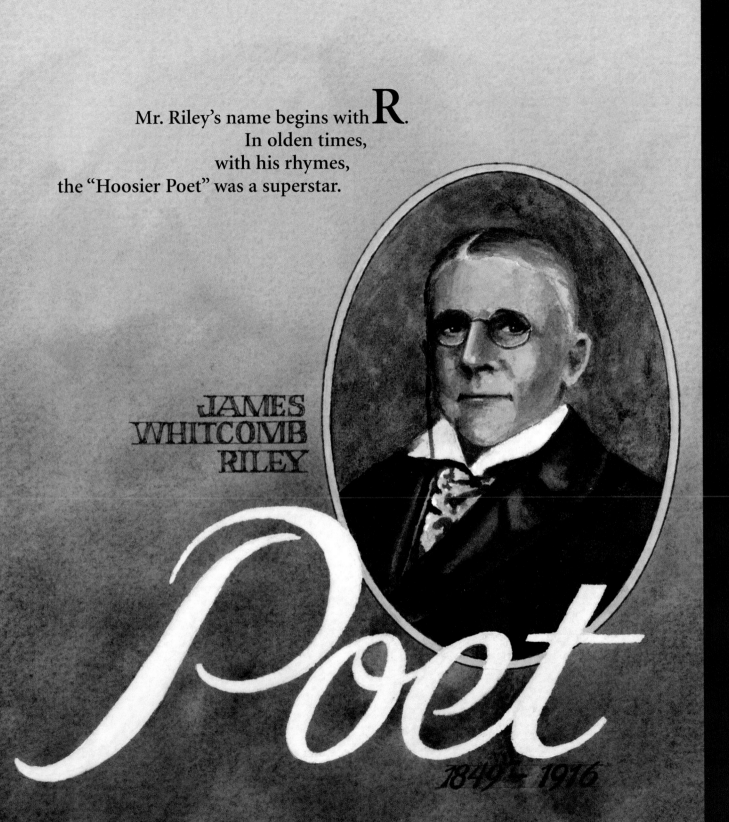

R r

Mr. Riley's name begins with **R**.
In olden times,
with his rhymes,
the "Hoosier Poet" was a superstar.

JAMES
WHITCOMB
RILEY

Poet

1849 – 1916

Known as the "Hoosier Poet," James Whitcomb Riley was born in Greenfield in 1849. He wrote poems about his childhood memories in Hoosier dialect with cheerful, fun-loving humor. His early poems appeared in the *Indianapolis Journal* under the pen name of "Benj. F Johnson, of Boone." These poems were collected in *The Old Swimmin' Hole and 'Leven More Poems*.

One of Mr. Riley's famous poems is *Little Orphant Annie* which inspired the comic strip *L'il Orphan Annie*. Another famous poem, "The Raggedy Man," was the inspiration for two rag dolls named "Raggedy Ann" and "Raggedy Andy."

Indiana has also been home to other great writers: Ernie Pyle, Booth Tarkington, Charles and Mary Beard, Theodore Dreiser, Lew Wallace, Gene Stratton Porter, and Kurt Vonnegut.

In 1816, Indiana became the first state to write a constitution that provided free statewide public schools. However, there was no tax money to pay for those schools until 1849.

The first school buildings were log cabins built by parents of schoolchildren. Potbelly stoves heated the schoolroom and dried wet clothes for children who walked to school in the snow or rain. Students were responsible for cleaning and decorating the school, keeping the stove full of wood, tutoring younger students, and carrying buckets of drinking water.

One teacher would teach children of all ages reading, writing, and arithmetic, as well as the Golden Rule ("Do unto others as you would have them do unto you"). In the beginning to save paper, students used slates. Since other books were scarce, Bibles were used for reading lessons. Older boys and girls missed school if they were needed to work on the farm.

Ready for the next letter?
The alphabet gets better and better!

S sits at the head of the word School.
In olden days, schools taught the Golden Rule.
Reading, writing and 'rithmetic were practiced on slates,
and students memorized poems and important dates.

Tt

Indiana's official state tree is the tulip tree, also known as the yellow poplar. When you look closely, you will see large, broad leaves and yellowish tulip-shaped flowers with an orange stamen in the center.

There are two kinds of tulip trees: one with yellow edges on its leaves and one with rounded green edges. Its twigs smell spicy.

This tree can grow up to 200 feet tall and as much as 10 feet thick at its base. Woodworkers like to work with the yellow wood.

Tulip trees are relics of an ancient geological age. Once they covered all of North America and Europe. Now they are only found in the eastern half of the United States and also in China.

T T The next letter we see is T.
T stands tall for the Tulip Tree.
Named for its yellow, tulip-shaped flowers,
this tree grows big, so you can play in its shade for hours.

Begun in 1804, the Underground Railroad was a network of people called "conductors," who guided slaves from the South to freedom in Canada. They stopped at hiding places called "stations" that often displayed a secret "signal," such as a gourd by the door or a light in the window.

Hoosiers were exceptionally active in the Underground Railroad because nearby Kentucky was a slave state. The Newport (now Fountain City) home of Levi and Catharine Coffin was called "Grand Central Station" because more than 2,000 slaves stopped there on their way to freedom—and not one was caught! Harriet Beecher Stowe used the Coffins as models for Simeon and Rachel Halliday in her book *Uncle Tom's Cabin*.

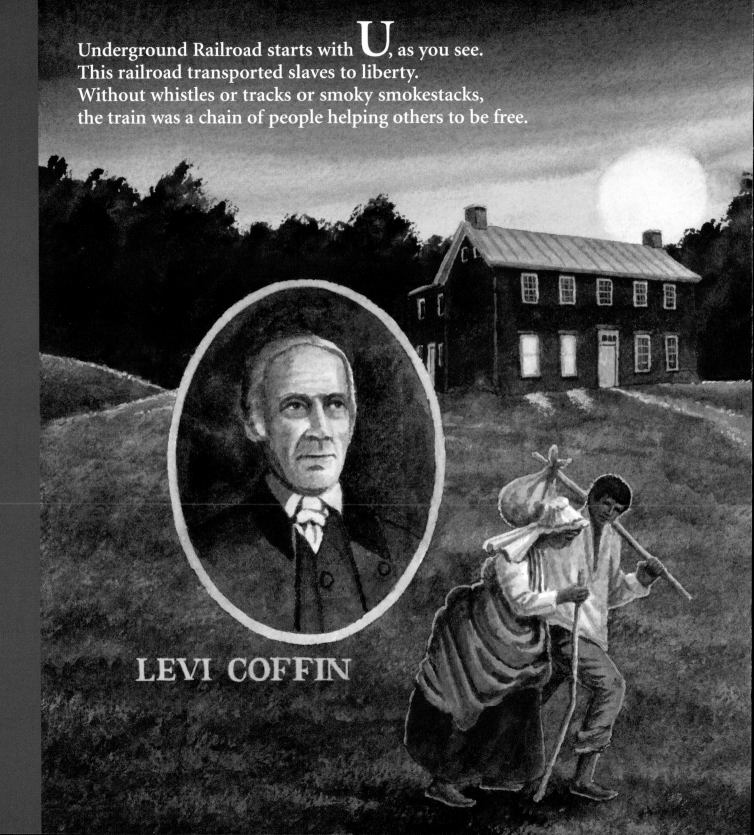

Underground Railroad starts with U, as you see.
This railroad transported slaves to liberty.
Without whistles or tracks or smoky smokestacks,
the train was a chain of people helping others to be free.

LEVI COFFIN

Read all about it!
Vincennes begins with V,
home of our first newspaper
and first public library.

GEORGE
RODGERS
CLARK

V
V

Exciting adventures in Indiana's history took place in Vincennes. First established as a French trading post in 1700, Vincennes was the site of a great American victory over the British during the American Revolution. Later, from 1800 until 1813, it was Indiana Territory's first capital city.

Vincennes is where Indiana's first newspaper, the *Indiana Gazette* (now the *Vincennes Sun-Commercial*), was printed in 1804, and where the state's first public library opened in 1807.

Vincennes' capture by George Rogers Clark during the summer of 1778 has been called "one of the most heroic episodes in U.S. history." Twenty-five-year-old Lieutenant Clark and 175 other Americans captured British forts at Kaskaskia, Cahokia, and Vincennes. Even though the British sent more soldiers and retook Vincennes, Clark was able to recapture the fort in February 1779 after marching 180 miles through deep snow. The George Rogers Clark National Historic Park commemorates that victory.

W stands for Wyandotte Cave,
explored by people who are brave.
In passages far below the ground,
stalactites and stalagmites can be found.

Wyandotte Cave is one of the largest natural limestone caves in the world! Here, deep beneath southern Indiana, you can see spectacular stalactites and stalagmites in the cave's 25 miles of underground passages and chambers.

A stalactite is a formation that hangs from the cave roof and looks like an icicle. It is made when mineral-rich ground water drips in the same area for a long time. A stalagmite grows from the cave floor up toward the ceiling. It too is made of mineral ground water. When stalactites and stalagmites grow together they form columns or pillars.

In Wyandotte Cave, you can see the Pillar of the Constitution, and two rooms called the Grand Cathedral and Senate Chamber.

Limestone, which is deposited deep beneath southern Indiana, is our state stone.

Indiana's state motto is "Crossroads of America" and, true to its motto, Indiana has more highways than any other state. We have nearly 92,000 miles of roads and more than 4,000 miles of railroad track. When you look at a map, you'll see why Indiana is called the "Crossroads of America."

The first east-west road to cross Indiana was the historic Cumberland Trail, also called the National Road (now U.S. Highway 40), which reached Indianapolis in 1834.

With so many roads and railroad crossings, it is important to "stop, look and listen" before you cross.

X is found at crossings
on roads across our state.
"Crossroads of America"—
this motto fits just great.

Y is for Yellow, a mellow yellow,
the color in which farmers' fields are dressed
during Indiana's autumn harvest,
when corn and soy crops are at their best.

Yellow is the color of Indiana in late summer and early autumn when a hot yellow sun lights up farmers' crops just before harvest. Ripening wheat turns from green to a soft, mellow yellow. Soybean plants launch bright yellow blooms. Stalks and tassels turn golden when corn ripens. Wherever you look in Indiana's countryside, you see yellow.

Neat-as-a-pin farms cover Indiana. Many were carved out of forests in the early 1800s—and many of them remain in the hands of their original families. Our state's 63,000 farms are part of America's Corn Belt; their average size is 246 acres.

Corn and soybeans are Indiana's leading crops. Corn is one of America's oldest crops, valued by Native Americans for thousands of years. Indiana grows one-fifth of all the corn used to make popcorn in the United States. Soybeans are fairly new to farmers' fields and are an important food source too.

ZIONSVILLE

And now, last but not least: **Z**.
Zionsville begins with **Z**.
In this small, charming village,
Hoosiers gathered to see
President Lincoln on his way to Washington, D.C.

In 1861, after he was elected president, Abraham Lincoln stopped in Zionsville to talk with the citizens on his way to the White House. Four years later, the president's funeral train sounded a sad, haunting whistle as it passed through town. Teary-eyed townspeople lined the railroad tracks that day.

Late in the 19th century, Zionsville became an important cultural center in the Midwest, where famous people came to listen, debate, and learn. Today, Zionsville looks much the way it did at that time.

Z Z

A Hoosier Wagon Full of Facts

1. Just what is a Hoosier? Are you one?

2. Who was the Hoosier Poet?

3. What does the word Indiana mean?

4. What is our state bird and what does he look like?

5. What is our state tree?

6. What community in Indiana was called the "Grand Central Station" of the Underground Railroad?

7. Who invented Indiana's favorite sport—and what is it?

8. Who wrote the state poem and what is its title?

9. Why is Elwood Haynes famous?

10. Which Great Lake is on Indiana's border?

11. What is the capital city of Indiana?

12. What is our state flower?

13. Who was the first governor of Indiana?

14. What astronaut was born in Indiana and has a museum named for him?

15. What three presidents lived in Indiana?

16. Where do Hoosiers like to spend Memorial Day?

17. What firsts are associated with the city of Vincennes?

18. Who was George Rogers Clark and why is he important?

19. What is the nickname for Indiana?

20. Where can you find stalactites and stalagmites in Indiana?

1. There is no tried-and-true answer to the question of what is a Hoosier, but you are one if you were born in Indiana or live here.

2. James Whitcomb Riley, born in a two-room log cabin in Greenfield in 1849, was called the Hoosier Poet because he wrote wonderful poems about old-fashioned boyhood adventures in Indiana.

3. Indiana means "Land of Indians." Twenty-three tribes lived on Indiana's lands through the centuries. Prehistoric relics tell us that the earliest natives lived here 15,000 years ago.

4. The cardinal is Indiana's state bird. Male birds have brilliant red coats with a thick orange-red bill. Females are a brownish-red.

5. There are more than 100 native species of trees in Indiana, but the official state tree is the tulip tree, which got its name because of its tulip-shaped leaves.

6. Fountain City was known as the Underground Railroad's "Grand Central Station" because so many slaves stopped here on their way to freedom in Canada.

7. Dr. James Naismith, a physical education teacher in Springfield, Massachusetts, invented the game of basketball in 1891.

8. Arthur Franklin Mapes of Kendallville wrote "Indiana," our state's official poem.

9. Elwood Haynes is famous for inventing the first gas-powered automobile.

10. Indiana's boundary runs along Lake Michigan for forty miles.

11. Indianapolis became our state capital in 1825 because it was centrally located in the heart of the Corn Belt. When Indiana entered the Union in 1816, however, Corydon was the capital.

12. The peony, which blooms with a wonderful fragrance in spring, is Indiana's state flower.

13. Jonathan Jennings was our first governor and the man most responsible for helping Indiana become a state.

14. Virgil ("Gus") Grissom was born in Mitchell and trained as a military pilot before becoming a member of the first team of astronauts to fly for the United States. You can tour the Grissom Air Museum in Bunker Hill.

15. Indiana was the boyhood home of Abraham Lincoln, our 16th president served from 1861-1865. Indiana also sent two Harrisons to the White House: William Henry Harrison in 1841, and his grandson, Benjamin Harrison in 1889.

16. Hoosiers flock to the Indianapolis Motor Speedway to watch the Indianapolis 500 automobile race.

17. Vincennes was the Indiana Territory's first capital city. Here, Indiana's first news-paper, the *Indiana Gazette*, was printed, and Vincennes opened Indiana's first public library.

18. George Rogers Clark captured the British fort at Vincennes during the American Revolution—and then recaptured the fort after the British reclaimed it. Historians assert that the battle was "one of the most heroic episodes in U.S. history" because it ensured American claims to the Indiana territory after the war.

19. Indiana is known as the "Crossroads of America" because it has always been a gateway to the West and South and because more highways run through Indiana than any other state.

20. Stalactites and stalagmites can be found in many limestone caves in southern Indiana, especially Wyandotte Cave.